FULL-CONTACT
KARATE

FULL-CONTACT KARATE

JEAN YVES THERIAULT
PKA Middleweight World Champion
WITH JOSEPH JENNINGS

CONTEMPORARY
BOOKS, INC.
CHICAGO

Library of Congress Cataloging in Publication Data

Theriault, Jean Yves.
   Full-contact karate.

   Includes index.
   1. Karate.   2. Jennings, Joseph.   II. Title.
GV1114.3.T53   1982   796.8'153   82-22191
ISBN 0-8092-5597-9

Published by Contemporary Books, Inc.
180 North Michigan Avenue, Chicago, Illinois 60601
Manufactured in the United States of America
Library of Congress Catalog Card Number: 82-22191
International Standard Book Number: 0-8092-5597-9

Published simultaneously in Canada by
Beaverbooks, Ltd.
150 Lesmill Road
Don Mills, Ontario M3B 2T5
Canada

Special thanks to my beautiful wife, Suzanne, whose constant support and inspiration helped make my dreams come true.

To John Therien, my manager and best friend, whose hard work and guidance has made me one of the sport's most successful fighters.

And to my family, friends, and fans, whose cheers I will always cherish.

Jean Yves Theriault

To my sisters Lucille, Mary Ann, Dolores, and Flora Ann.

Joseph Jennings

contents

acknowledgments

The authors would like to express their appreciation to photographers Tom Evans and Myles Burke for contributing so many fine action photos to the book.

To Victor Theriault for assisting in many of the instructional photographs.

To Mr. Don Quine of the Professional Karate Association and Inside Kung-Fu magazine for supplying important information concerning the sports history and rules.

And to Carole Smith for her help in preparing the manuscript.

Knocking out PKA light heavyweight contender Kerry Roop of Detroit, Michigan, in the fifth round April 19, 1979, at the Ottawa Civic Center, Ottawa, Canada. Photo by Armand Legault.

chapter one

introduction

No sport has come as far, in such a short time, as professional full-contact karate. Developed in the early 1970s, this exciting sport exploded on the world sporting scene in September 1974, when it was featured on television for the first time in a 90-minute special on ABC's "Wide World of Entertainment." This historic event, presented by Universal Television and sanctioned by the Professional Karate Association (PKA), featured 14 fighters from eight countries. When it was over, the following athletes emerged as world champions in this new nonstop action combat sport: Joe Lewis, heavyweight (USA); Jeff Smith, light heavyweight (USA); Bill "Superfoot" Wallace, middleweight (USA); and Isaias Duenas, lightweight (Mexico).

The PKA championships on national television captured the hearts of millions of fight fans as they witnessed fighters using

1

their feet as well as their hands for the knockout. In fact, the spectator response was so great that the show received the highest rating recorded in its time slot for two years.

Such early enthusiasm continues and grows stronger every day as PKA full-contact karate is now seen almost weekly on national TV. It is aired regularly on ABC, CBS, NBC, and ESPN, the all-sports cable network. The major networks have broadcast more than 30 PKA fights nationally, most of which have been seen around the world via satellite. Combined ratings to date total 100,000,000 TV viewers for PKA full-contact karate, not including weekly cable audiences. Through such exposure it is fast becoming one of the world's leading spectator sports. PKA karate is truly the kick of the future!

The sport's quick growth and popularity can be attributed to its sanctioning and founding body, the Professional Karate Association. Based in California and spearheaded by the tireless efforts of cofounders Don and Judy Quine and Joe Corley, Coordinator of International Events, the PKA has created and developed the standardized rules governing PKA-sanctioned full-contact karate. These rules include the minimum kicking requirements, now eight per round, imposed to keep fighters from using punching tactics alone.

The state athletic commissions, which regulate professional and amateur boxing and wrestling in many states, began regulating contact karate in 1976. This marked the first time in America that an authorized government body administered any form of martial arts. The California State Athletic Commission was the first to recognize PKA's rules and policies as the standards for the sport. In July 1978 the North American Boxing Federation, to which all state athletic commissions belong, approved a motion to recognize the PKA officially as the international governing body of professional full-contact karate. Following that development, the PKA established and now maintains worldwide ratings of fighters, thereby validating continental and world champion titles.

As rough-and-tumble as the sport appears, none of its fighters competing under PKA-sanctioned events has ever been mortally

Full-contact karate's nonstop action and its weekly coverage on national TV has made it one of the world's most popular and exciting spectator sports. Photo by Myles Burke.

PKA fight coordinator and ex-karate point champion Joe Corley interviews a full-contact karate fighter after a hard-fought PKA televised bout on NBC. Photo by Joe Benton.

or seriously injured. This can be attributed to the PKA's strict enforcement and development of rules designed to protect the fighters. Full-contact karate is not a free-for-all brawl in which fighters can let go with anything. It is a very technical and tactical contact sport in which only certain techniques are allowed and should not be confused with or compared to the Asian art of Japanese and Thai kickboxing, in which fighters wear little protective equipment and are allowed to batter each other with everything from elbows to knees with little regard for their safety.

4

PKA full-contact karate makes a great effort to disassociate itself from Asian, Japanese, and Thai kickboxing, in which fighters wear little protective equipment and are allowed to kick to the legs and employ deadly knee and elbow strikes. PKA fighters are required to wear protective kicking boots and fight under strict rules to protect competitors from senseless injuries. Photos left and above courtesy of Joseph Jennings.

WHY FULL-CONTACT KARATE?

Full-contact karate grew out of the traditional semi- or no-contact point karate tournaments held regularly throughout the United States and Canada since the early 1960s. These events required fighters to control and pull their strikes to avoid making hard contact with their opponents. Some fighters who participated in these "tag" matches did not feel that they represented a true test of their abilities and began asking promoters to develop a separate division for those competitors who were willing to go at it full blast to see who would be the victor. Many promoters agreed to these fighters' requests, and thus full-contact karate was born.

Full-contact karate has changed drastically since its early days. Early fighters fought in ropeless rings, using the same four-ounce safety gloves worn by semi-contact point fighters. Many of the point fighters who converted to the full-contact version did so without proper preparation, appearing preposterously unconditioned, with some fighters unable to get through three two-minute rounds. Many thought the only transition you had to make to full-contact from semi-contact events was to hit full force instead of pulling your techniques. This myth was soon discarded as point fighters quickly realized that full-contact was a whole new sport, for which conditioning and months of hard training were needed to survive.

Today's full-contact karate fighters are superathletes and are improving all the time as they discover the techniques that win in this demanding sport. I feel very fortunate that I can share my knowledge and contribute to fighters' development through the publication of this book—a source that I wish had been available to me when I started in this sport.

Written from experience, this book will help you eliminate hours of wasted training time and put you on the road to victory much more quickly than you could expect without it. The success formula presented here, one that has taken me to the PKA world Middleweight title, is a simple one that stresses hard conditioning and the perfection and use of basic techniques. I strongly believe in developing basic powerful techniques that get the job done rather than wasting a moment's time on flashy movements that look great but are ineffective when it comes to taking care of your opponent.

GETTING STARTED

In your quest to study full-contact karate you may find it hard to locate a gym that teaches the sport in your area. However, you can get this important information from the PKA's Associated School Program, which lists schools and gyms involved in teaching the sport worldwide. Write to the PKA Associated School Program, 2930 Hutton Dr., Beverly Hills, CA 90210. Demand for gyms currently outweighs availability because this is still a relatively young sport. But don't let this discourage you; there are several ways to get involved.

If you are unable to find a full-contact karate gym in your area, take the following approach, which is similar to the way I started.

Since the kicking skills are those of karate and the hand techniques come from boxing, you may have to seek the services of both types of schools. Visit the karate and boxing gyms in your area and thoroughly discuss your goals as a full-contact fighter with the gyms' teachers and trainers. If they approve of your goals and are willing to help, you should begin your training first in a karate school because you will find the kicks harder to develop than the punches. Your traditional karate training will also give you the discipline to work hard and help develop your reflexes and balance. You should expect to study for a minimum of six months, concentrating on perfecting four basic kicks—the front, side, hook, and roundhouse. Do not be concerned with receiving karate belt ranks, because in full-contact karate belts are not required as in no-contact traditional karate schools. Black belts are worn by full-contact fighters during a match only as a way to help distinguish karate from other forms of fighting such as Japanese and Thai kickboxing. I myself acquired only a yellow belt in jujitsu and traditional karate before making the transition to full-contact karate.

With your kicking skills perfected, begin training at a boxing gym to develop your punching skills. Through boxing training and sparring sessions you will learn footwork and slipping maneuvers, you will learn to take a punch, and you will understand the importance of conditioning. Although you won't be able to throw kicks when sparring you can start putting together kick, punch combinations on the heavy bag.

TRAINERS AND MANAGERS

After you have established a foundation in the sport you should seek out a competent trainer and manager who are willing to invest time and money in the development of your career. (Although these jobs are usually handled by two different people, sometimes a trainer will double as your manager if he has the knowledge and time to do so.)

The best trainer is one who is or was an experienced fighter, whether in traditional point karate, in full-contact karate, or in boxing. A man who talks from experience can better develop your fight strategy and relate to every aspect of your training. Your trainer will bring out the best in you through his demand for hard work and discipline, which assures victory and keeps you from getting hurt.

You must be able to trust your trainer and your manager 100 percent. There may be times when you disagree with your trainer, but always listen to him for his knowledge and make it a point to keep in harmony with him.

While your trainer develops you as a fighter, your manager works to get you the fights and purses you deserve. I am very fortunate to be managed by John Therien, the PKA's representative for Canada, and one of the top managers in the sport. He has guided my career from the amateur to the pro level, to the point at which I am now one of the highest-paid fighters in the sport's history, a position I never could have achieved alone. Managers make the right decisions for the advancement of your career by taking care of all major and minor details, from signing the fight contract to making your hotel reservations. A good manager does everything he can so that his fighter is not distracted and can devote all his time to training.

The manager will normally finance your expenses in return for a percentage of your purses over a certain length of time. This arrangement is usually structured by a written contract, which you should always discuss thoroughly with your attorney before signing.

With purses currently averaging from $5,000 to $20,000 per championship fight and rising, the potential for making a living in PKA full-contact karate is looking better every year. A champ averages four fights a year to defend his title, with a couple of nontitle bouts thrown in. At this point in time, only top fighters earn the big bucks and can therefore afford to devote all their

A fighter's career is a team effort. I could never have made it to the top without the help of my manager, John Therien (right), and trainer Guy Malette (left).

time to the sport and not have to work at another job. In the coming years, I'm sure that all PKA fighters will be able to make a great living in the sport.

To reach such a lofty position will not be easy and will require a tremendous amount of hard work and sacrifice. You must also be motivated to succeed in a sport that demands long-term commitments to courage, sacrifice, and plenty of sweat.

Before turning pro, you should make it a point to talk to other pros you respect. Their insight will help you decide on making a commitment.

Photo by Tom Evans.

chapter two

highlights of PKA
rules and regulations

RULES AND PROCEDURES

As a full-contact karate fighter it is very important that you familiarize yourself with the rules, regulations, and procedures of the sport so you can develop your fight strategy accordingly, especially when you move from amateur to pro status.

A large number of rules listed in the Professional Karate Association's 22-page official rules and regulations manual are akin to those used in pro boxing. Listed here is a synopsis of some rules applying exclusively to PKA full-contact karate. Because the sport is relatively new, the PKA rules and procedures have been revised nine times since their inception in 1975, with the main concern always being the safety and protection of the full-contact karate fighter.

Use of these rules does not necessarily imply sanction of competition by the Professional Karate Association. Such sanction must be arranged specifically with the PKA, and the association's name may not be used unless a formal sanction agreement has been entered into. Inquiries should be addressed to Professional Karate Association, Sanctions Director, 2930 Hutton Dr., Beverly Hills, CA 90210.

The Ring

The ring shall be a regulation boxing ring not less than 16 square feet within the ropes. The ring floor shall extend beyond the ropes not less than 18 inches. The ring floor shall be padded, and padding must extend beyond the ring ropes and over the edge of the platform. The ring platform shall not be more than four feet above the floor. The ropes are to be padded and shall be a minimum of three in number and not less than one inch in diameter.

Equipment

In addition to boxing gloves, fighters wear foot pads covering the tops and sides of their feet and leaving the soles of the feet bare. Foot wrapping designations correspond to hand wraps used in both boxing and full-contact. Eight-ounce gloves are used for welterweight and lighter divisions, 10-ounce gloves for heavier classes.

Length of Rounds and Duration of Matches

Rounds are two minutes long with rests of one minute. Pro fights are not less than five rounds; amateur bouts may be three, four, or five rounds in length. The required length of pro title fights is:

State Title Fights:	7 rounds
Regional Title Fights:	8 rounds

National or Continental: 9 rounds
World Title Fights: 12 rounds

Nine two-minute rounds of full-contact karate have been measured by stress and trauma physicians to equal the energy utilized in fifteen three-minute rounds of boxing. This is due to the added energy expended by fighters mandated to execute a minimum of eight above-the-waist kicks in each two-minute round. World title fights were nine rounds long until 1977, when the current 12-round duration was adopted.

Authorized Offensive Techniques

These include certain full-contact punches such as ridge hands and spinning backfists, as well as classic boxing punches. They also include kicking above the waist and sweeps executed boot to boot only.

Fouls

Full-contact, unlike Japanese or Thai kickboxing, does not permit head butting, striking with elbows or knees, or striking to the groin. No kicks below the waist are allowed, thus kicking to the legs is also forbidden. Grabbing or holding the leg is a foul, as is legchecking—extending the leg to check an opponent's leg to prevent him from kicking.

Minimum Kick Rule—Minimum Kicking Requirement

Each contestant must execute a minimum of eight kicking techniques during the course of each round. The kicks must be clear attempts to make contact with the opponent in a legal target area. If a fighter does not execute his minimum kicking requirements (MKRs), he will automatically be penalized two points on each judge's scorecard for each kick less than eight that he executed.

Elbow strikes.

Knee strikes.

Groin strikes.

Checking or kicking the legs.

16

If a fighter fails to execute his MKRs in any two rounds of a three- to eight-round bout, the bout will be stopped and the victory awarded to his opponent. If a fighter fails to execute his MKRs in any three rounds of a nine- to twelve-round bout, he will automatically be disqualified and the victory awarded to his opponent. If both fighters miss their MKRs for two or three rounds, as described above, the fight is declared a technical draw. The public address announcer will inform the audience of all MKR violations.

Minimum Kick Rule Officials

The MKR official assigned to count the kicks thrown per round by Fighter A sits opposite Fighter A's corner; the official counting Fighter B's kicks per round sits opposite his corner. Both officials hold flip cards, numbered 1–20, flipping to the next number as each qualified kick is thrown. An MKR official records the total number of kicks executed by the fighter he is counting on an MKR ballot at the conclusion of each round (even if the number exceeds 20). Should a fighter not meet his MKR of eight kicks in any round, the MKR official notifies the referee of the number thrown. The referee then notifies the scorekeeper, who records the appropriate penalty. Failure to meet MKRs, the penalty assessed, and the possible consequences are announced on the PA before the start of the next round.

Scoring

Three judges vote, marking individual signed ballots after each round. A 10-point must system (one of the fighters must receive a full 10 points at the end of each round), is used, and ballots are collected at the round's conclusion by the assistant scorekeeper. The scorekeeper records points from each of the ballots, deposits ballots in a locked box, then deducts foul points as instructed by the referee. Thus the scorekeeper tabulates these results on the master scoresheet. At the conclusion of the bout the scorekeeper

17

makes the final tally. the PKA representative verifies each fighter's final score from the locked ballots and reports the results, including each fighter's total kick count, to the referee and house announcer.

WEIGHTS AND CLASSES

Bantamweight	118–124.9 lbs.
Super-Lightweight	125–132.9 lbs.
Lightweight	133–140.9 lbs.
Super-Welterweight	141–147.9 lbs.
Welterweight	148–155.9 lbs.
Super-Middleweight	156–163.9 lbs.
Middleweight	164–171.9 lbs.
Light-Heavyweight	172–180.9 lbs.
Heavyweight	181–194.9 lbs.
Name to be determined	over 195 lbs.

The following weight spread is permissible for matchmaking within each weight division. Any greater weight spread requires the approval of the PKA.

Bantamweight	not more than 4 lbs.
Super-Lightweight	not more than 5 lbs.
Lightweight	not more than 6 lbs.
Welterweight	not more than 7 lbs.
Middleweight	not more than 8 lbs.
Light-Heavyweight	not more than 9 lbs.
Heavyweight	no limit
Name to be determined	no limit

WEIGHING TIME

Contestants will be weighed on or before the day of the match, at a time to be determined by the PKA or the promoter, in the presence of a PKA representative, on scales approved by the PKA. By special permission of the PKA, preliminary fighters

18

highlights of pka rules and regulations

may be allowed to weigh in and be examined not later than one hour before the scheduled time of the first bout of the program. All weights are done when stripped.

Photo by Tom Evans.

chapter three

conditioning for confidence

Having traveled all over the world giving seminars on full-contact karate, I have found that the majority of amateur and pro fighters are lacking most in three areas: (1) conditioning, (2) balance and footwork, and (3) adequate defense.

If you were to ask anyone seriously involved in pugilistic sports—whether it be boxing, wrestling, or full-contact karate—how important conditioning is, he would respond without hesitation that conditioning is everything. Nothing could be more true. A well-conditioned fighter is a confident fighter capable of taking blows and going the distance.

Because it uses the entire body as a fighting machine, full-contact karate makes tremendous demands on one's physical abilities. Therefore, it is truly a sport in which only the strong survive, a sport dominated by fighters who have the discipline to train religiously.

A well-conditioned fighter is able to take blows without injury and has the endurance to go the distance. Photo by Myles Burke.

Getting in top physical condition is a lonely, hard journey that can be accomplished only through strong mental motivation. If you want to be victorious in full-contact karate, you must will yourself to respond to your training and completely give in to the necessary stress and work entailed in such a challenging endeavor. To think failure is most assuredly to fail to maximize your full potential as a fighter. You must have complete confidence in your training routine in order to gain the most from it. Attack each workout with great enthusiasm and determination.

The following exercises and training routines will get you in the best shape of your life, enabling you to perform the techniques in the following chapters with competence as well as preparing you for your first fight. Perform them in the general order shown.

If you have no prior training in full-contact karate, it is wise to see a physician to have a complete physical before you proceed with the following training routines. When performing exercises, only put forth what you are capable of handling until you can get in shape to perform the minimum repetitions suggested.

It is not as much the amount of the exercise you are performing as the quality and intensity of each repetition that makes the exercises beneficial. Do each exercise with strict form and total concentration. Ten good push-ups are worth as much as fifty sloppy ones.

GYM TRAINING GEAR

For training in the club, shorts or sweat pants should be worn with a loose fitting T-shirt to absorb sweat. Always wear sneakers when training, except for sparring, when safety boots are worn.

OVERTRAINING—A BEGINNER'S MISTAKE

Overtraining in full-contact karate can have the same negative effect as not training enough. Overtraining is likely to plague novices within the first two months of training. It is usually caused by an overzealous desire to train beyond your structured routine, based on the attitude that more is better. This obviously is not always true, because doing too much and not giving the body substantial time to rest and rebuild between workouts often gives the fighter a feeling of "flatness," which results in mental and physical depression and often muscular injury due to exhaustion and the inability to concentrate during training. Be aware of any of these symptoms in yourself; they are all vital signs of overtraining.

To overcome feeling fatigued, listen carefully to your body. If it is overworked, do not be afraid to take a day or two off to regain your energy and enthusiasm.

WARM-UPS

The following simple but effective warm-up exercises are essential to stepping up circulation, stretching certain muscles, improving mobility, and preparing the body for the vigorous demands of the training session to follow. They also aid you in

23

increasing your awareness of your muscular needs in preparation for an exercise and in reducing the potential for pulls and strains. Avoid rushing through your warm-ups; do them thoroughly to get the maximum benefit.

1. neck stretch
2. hip stretch
3. side bends
4. torso rotations
5. body twist

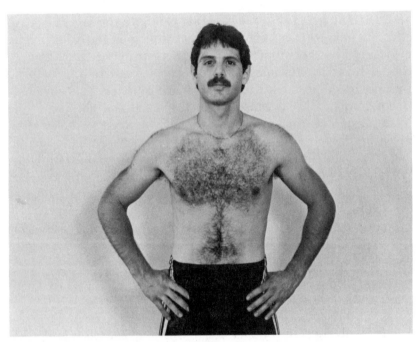

NECK STRETCH: To limber up the neck muscles for quicker mobility and to avoid pinched nerves when the head is turned sharply, use this stretch. Start by placing your hands on your hips.

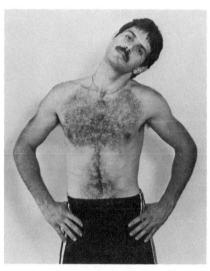 

Stretch your neck to the left for a count of five, keeping your shoulders down.

Repeat to the right.

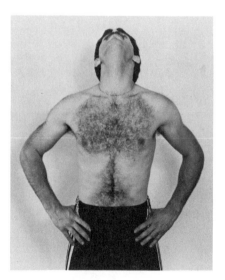 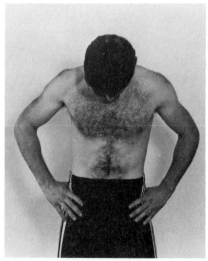

Pulling your chin up, stretch your head back.

Finish by stretching forward. Repeat 10 times.

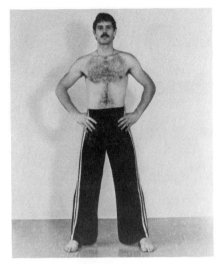

HIP STRETCH. Left: To loosen the hips for the performance of kicking techniques, use this hip stretch. Begin with your feet shoulder width apart, with your hands on your hips. Below, left: Keeping your torso straight, stretch your upper body to the left, concentrating on stretching your left hip. Below, right: Repeat to the right. Bottom, left: Stretch backward with your head up and your back straight. Bottom, right: End by stretching forward with the back straight. Repeat 10 times.

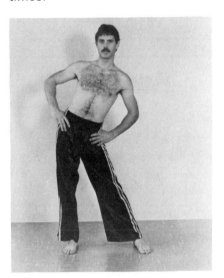

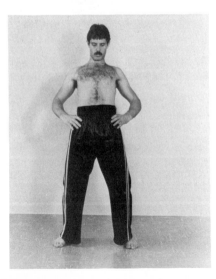

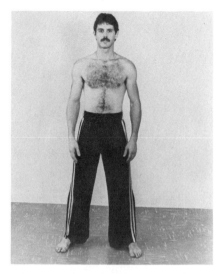

SIDE BENDS. Use this warm-up to loosen the shoulders and latissimus (back) muscles. Begin by standing relaxed with your hands down at your sides.

Placing your left hand on your left knee, raise your right arm and stretch to your left side.

Repeat to the other side, placing your right hand on your right knee and raising your left arm to stretch to the right. Do 10 repetitions on each side.

27

TORSO ROTATIONS. Right: Immediately follow your hip stretches and side bends with torso rotations. Begin by assuming a ready position with your hands on your hips and your feet spread shoulder width apart. Below, left: Drop down from the waist, rotating to your left and keeping your hands on your hips, with your back and head parallel to the floor. Below, right and bottom left and right: In a continuous motion, make a complete counterclockwise circle. Do 10 repetitions, alternating clockwise and counterclockwise rotations.

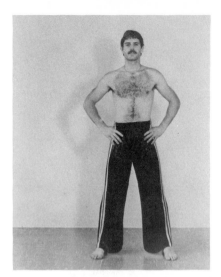

BODY TWIST. This warm-up prepares your back, shoulders, and hips. Begin by extending your arms out at your sides at shoulder height, parallel to the floor.

Swing your arms and twist sharply to the left, turning your hips with the movement.

Repeat to the right; perform 10 times.

STRETCHING

All sports requiring heavy use of the legs incorporate stretching exercises into their conditioning regimes for the prevention of pulled muscles and tendons and for greater flexibility. Because full-contact karate's extensive use of kicks is part of a fighter's arsenal of offensive and defensive techniques, an intense stretching regime is of the utmost importance. Flexible leg muscles will produce greater speed and balance in a fighter. Stretching should be performed for a minimum of 20 minutes before and 10 minutes after each running and training session. So, if you run in the morning and train in the afternoon on the same day, you will have stretched a total of four times.

When performing the following exercises, stay relaxed and try to hold each position for 30 seconds, attempting to stretch farther on each repetition. Avoid bouncing movements and concentrate on maintaining proper form.

1. lunging stretch
2. squat stretch
3. side split

4. seated split
5. stretch bar—front kick stretch
6. stretch bar—side kick stretch

LUNGING STRETCH. Left and above: This exercise works well for stretching the groin muscles and Achilles tendon. Flexibility in the Achilles tendon is important to prevent injuries in this area when running and kicking the heavy bag. With your legs far apart, lunge forward and lean heavily on your front leg, keeping the weight of your rear leg high on the ball of the foot (supported almost entirely by your toes). Hold this position for 30 seconds, alternating sides for four repetitions.

SQUAT STRETCH. The squat stretch is ideal for stretching the groin and hamstrings. With your legs far apart, squat down to one side, keeping your supporting foot flat on the ground and the out-stretched leg on the heel with your toes pulled back toward you. Concentrate on pushing your body weight down for 30 seconds. Repeat to the other side. Do a total of four repetitions, alternating sides. Photos by Tom Evans.

SIDE SPLIT. This is a valuable exercise for developing your side kick. Start with your legs spread to 70 percent of their full sideways extension. Hold this starting position for 30 seconds, keeping your hands on the floor for support.

Gradually work your feet apart until they have reached your maximum split.

Top: At this point, grab hold of your left leg, pulling your head in toward the leg and holding this position for 30 seconds. Center: Repeat to the right. Above: Then repeat to the center for 30 seconds, touching your elbows to the floor. Do three repetitions of the entire series.

34

SEATED SPLIT. After completing the last upright movement in the standing split series, immediately sit down
from the standing position, keeping your legs apart.

Using the same stretching techniques as in the standing
split series, twist to the right, grasping your leg and
holding your head to your knee for 30 seconds.

Repeat to the left.

Finish by stretching to the center, touching your head to the floor.

STRETCH BAR—FRONT KICK STRETCH. Finish all stretching routines on the stretching bar. Perform the front kick stretch by placing your heel on the bar, keeping the toes pulled back tightly toward you. With your knee locked, bring your head to your leg. Alternate legs for two repetitions, holding each rep for 30 seconds. Photo by Tom Evans.

STRETCH BAR—SIDE KICK STRETCH. Turning your side to the bar, place your leg on the bar with the foot in the blade position, as if executing a side kick. Hold for 30 seconds, then alternate for two repetitions with each leg. Photo by Tom Evans.

SQUAT KICKS

After you have completed all stretching exercises and before you begin hard kick training, it is a very good idea to perform a series of squat kicks to warm up the legs and knees thoroughly. Besides preventing injuries, this exercise puts you in the proper frame of mind for kicking.

Stand with your feet shoulder width apart and your hands clenched into fists and held at chin level, with your elbows bent and held in at your ribs. Then squat down as far as possible, feeling a good stretch in the knees and thighs.

Right: Spring up, thrusting a front kick to the face with 75 percent power. Below, left: Squat down again. Below, right: Repeat the kick with the opposite leg. Perform 15 repetitions with each leg.

RUNNING

It is impossible for a fighter to get into top physical condition without daily runs to build stamina and endurance. Besides building wind capacity, running also exercises the arms, chest, abdominals, legs, and internal organs.

Running should be done early in the morning after 20 minutes of stretching exercises. When running, you should dress in a jogging suit to keep warm and help the body sweat. Sweating cleanses the body of impurities. Your sneakers should be lightweight and flexible enough that you can easily bend them, touching toe to heel.

Distance is not as important as the *way* you run. *Run* the distance you have chosen; don't *jog*. When running, do so rhythmically with your shoulders and arms relaxed.

The secret to my development of powerful kicking techniques was including step running in my training routine. Step running came about because of the cold Canadian climate I live in. To escape the cold during the winter months I would have to run inside the Ottawa Civic Sports Center, around its top deck. One day, to break the monotony, I started running up and down its aisles, each of which had more than 1,000 steps. Those steps were brutal at first, but as I got used to them they became responsible for putting two inches of muscles on my thighs and doubling my kicking power.

Also consider incorporating step or hill running into your running routine every other day. Running steps every day is too fatiguing.

My five-day running routine is as follows: On the first day I run two miles, then hit the steps for numerous up-and-down runs, and then end with a two-mile run. On the following day I run one mile to warm up and then ten 100-yard wind sprints full-blast, resting no longer than 10 seconds between sprints and finishing with another one-mile run. This running routine is severe and will take at least one year of training to accomplish. Always end your running with 20 minutes of stretching exercises and rest at least four hours after your morning run before starting your training in the gym to let your body recuperate completely.

A WORD ON DIET

As in a high-performance car, the fuel you burn will have a significant effect on your performance as an athlete. Since full-contact karate is a high-energy sport in which hundreds of calories are burned in a single workout, proper nutrition is necessary to keep up with its fast pace. Since "action energy" is derived from a conversion of muscle glycogen, which comes from carbohydrates in food, I eat a high-carbohydrate diet consisting mainly of pastas, bread, potatoes, natural fruits, and salads, with my proteins coming from fresh seafood and poultry products. I eat little red meat and no greasy foods because they make me sluggish since they take too long to digest.

While eating carbohydrates, it is important to remember to take plenty of fluids so that the carbohydrates can be stored in the muscles and not just passed through the body. Note that increasing your carbohydrate intake does not give you a license to overindulge. Keep your food consumption under control at all times, eating amounts that fill you comfortably, not stuff you, or you may find yourself in a higher weight division.

I find that two meals a day are sufficient for me, and I recommend waiting three to four hours after eating before you work out. You should feel a tinge of hunger before you begin a training session, but never train on an empty stomach; it will only lead to fatigue and nausea.

Multiple vitamins should also be taken once a day after your main meal to replace nutrients lost during training.

Proper rest also goes hand in hand with good nutrition. Getting the proper amount of sleep every day will work wonders toward keeping your energy level high. Spending all your nights partying will never bring you a championship title.

41

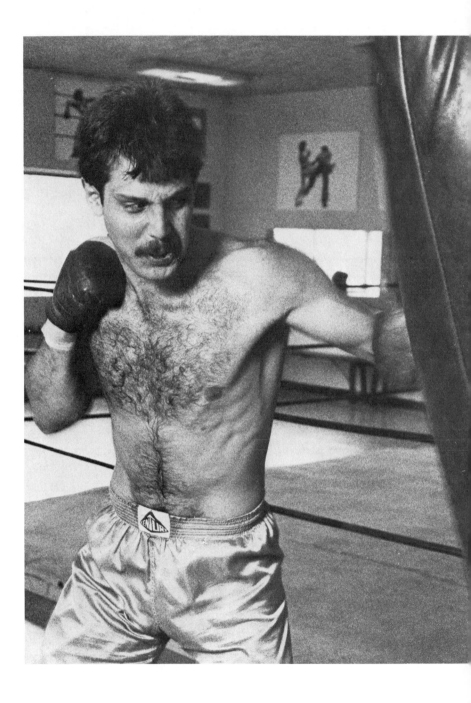

chapter four

full-contact training

After you have completed your morning run, stretching, and warm-up exercises, featured in the previous chapter, you are ready to begin your full-contact training routine. Since a variety of equipment is needed, including a ring, mirrors, a heavy bag, hand mitts, a speed ball, a medicine ball, and protective sparring gear, a well-equipped gym is essential.

TRAINING TIPS

For success in developing as a fighter, incorporate the following points into each workout.

1. Always train with a mouthpiece in to get used to breathing with it correctly.

2. Even though full-contact karate matches are two minutes in duration, with a minute's rest, work up to training for three-minute rounds in the gym for each exercise. This will give you the

physical advantage over your opponent of greater stamina and endurance.

3. Get into the habit of training at the same time for each workout; your body will respond more successfully to a standard regime rather than to a sporadic one.

4. Speed builds power; therefore, always put maximum speed behind your punching and kicking techniques in training.

5. The major role of the mind in creating a winning fighter cannot be stressed enough. Your mind has the power to give you the will to push on and become stronger when physically you feel you have nothing left. If two fighters are of equal ability, the one with the more determined mental attitude to win will succeed. Psyching yourself up for victory begins not on the day of a bout, but rather in each training session leading up to that day. When training, your mental image should depict you defeating your opponent and having your arm raised in triumph. This mental attitude is my key to success and is sure to do the same for you. Remember, the way you train is the way you will perform in the ring. If you train with victory in mind, you will realize victory in competition.

WRAPPING THE HANDS

Your hands should be wrapped carefully before each sparring session, just as for competition. Wrapping protects the knuckles from bruising and keeps the wrist secure, making it less susceptible to strains. I find that standard hand wraps are too short for the wrapping I prefer, so I sew two of them together for extra length. You may also find that this will work better for you.

When wrapping, put the starting loop around your thumb, working the strap first around your wrist, crossing the palm, and then between the fingers, ending with turns around the palm and wrist again. After the hands are wrapped, apply tape over them to keep the fist tight and firm. Be careful not to wrap so tightly that the circulation is cut off.

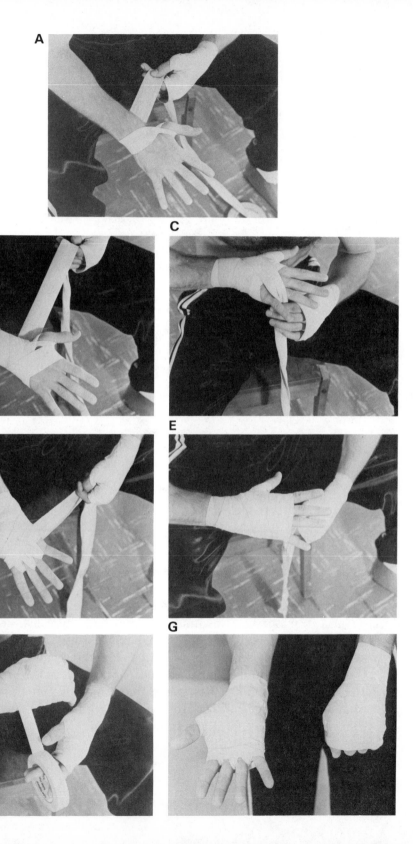

SHADOWBOXING

Shadowboxing is the first exercise performed in a training routine to help loosen the body and improve your footwork and rhythm. It is done in two ways—in front of a mirror to check your form and in the ring to simulate a real fight by working off the ropes and corners. When shadowboxing, stay relaxed and in constant motion, moving forward, back, and laterally, while executing offensive and defensive attacks and counters. Although you are striking only air, don't daydream; always react by pretending that an imaginary foe is in front of you. To build knockout power, strike with perfect form and blinding speed.

HEAVY BAG

Rounds on the bag are your most important power-building exercise. When working kicks and punches on the bag, avoid being stationary. Move around as if facing an actual opponent, constantly circling and pushing the bag. Strike as the bag swings at you and away from you to improve your distancing for offensive and defensive techniques. Work the bag with a variety of combinations to the midsection and head, hitting it full-power each time by putting your body weight behind each technique. Although the photos demonstrate this move using safety kicks, always wear sneakers when kicking the bag to protect the foot.

HAND MITTS

There is no greater piece of equipment for developing your punching skills than the hand mitts. They perfect your accuracy, reflexes, and footwork. Working in the ring, have your partner hold one mitt in each hand and move about the ring as if fighting an opponent, constantly shifting the mitts to bring out all your punches. For example, if your partner holds one high and one low, you are required to throw a punch to the body and head. Go for speed, striking as fast as possible with no less than a two-punch flurry per execution. Your partner should act defensively and offensively, moving away from and at you to test your footwork and to check your distancing to see if your techniques connect solidly. Work some rounds on the mitts by going through slipping maneuvers, as described in Chapter 8, before punching to improve your defensive tactics.

Where the heavy bag develops power, the hand mitts promote kicking speed and accuracy. With your partner holding a mitt in each hand, perform rounds by having him stay stationary as you strike with a variety of kicks to the head and midsection area.

SPEED BALL

This unique piece of training equipment is a leather ball about the size of a basketball, filled with air and attached to the floor and ceiling with a flexible cord. It is ideal for developing sharp reflexes, because, when struck, the ball moves in unpredictable directions, much the way an opponent will react. It takes great concentration to hit it consistently. Work the speed ball for at least two three-minute rounds per training session.

MEDICINE BALL KICKING

Besides its use as a body toughener, the medicine ball is used for kick training exercises. With your partner holding the ball at midsection level, execute your front, side, and roundhouse kicks into the ball full-power for a minimum of 15 repetitions with each leg.

A

B

C

ROPE SKIPPING

Rope skipping should be included in every workout to build stamina, rhythm, agility, and footwork. The main point to remember when starting out is to skip by rotating the rope with your wrists, keeping the elbows in at your sides. This will keep the rope consistently at one height to clear your feet and head. People have difficulty learning to skip rope when they make the mistake of trying to rotate the rope with their arms, which only shortens it, thus causing the rope to hit their head and feet.

MEDICINE BALL TOSS

Another good arm-strengthening routine is to hold your arms above your head and toss a 20-pound medicine ball back and forth with your partner. Do 20 repetitions.

MEDICINE BALL TRAINING

The midsection area can be toughened to withstand strikes through sit-ups and with the use of the medicine ball. Heavy ball training also builds your confidence so that you can hold your ground.

Above: With your partner standing approximately five feet from you, have him toss the medicine ball straight at your stomach. Below: Tighten your muscles on impact and catch the ball on its way down. Do 25 repetitions.

53

Above: To toughen the sides of the midsection, stand with one arm held high. Below: Have the ball thrown into the rib cage area. Tighten your muscles on impact and repeat 25 times.

MUSCULATURE EXERCISES

I end each training session with the following exercises, which are perfect for toning, toughening, and strengthening the upper body.

1. push-ups
2. tricep push-ups
3. sit-ups

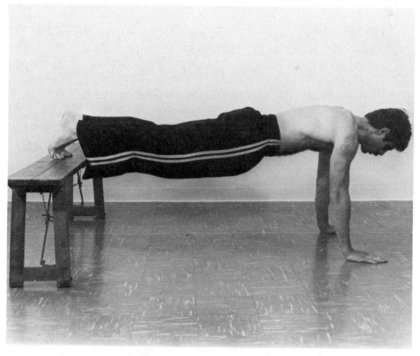

PUSH-UPS. To increase shoulder and arm strength for punching, begin by elevating your feet on a bench with your hands flat on the floor, shoulder width apart.

Keeping your back and legs straight, lower your body evenly until your face is one inch from the floor. Do 25 repetitions per workout.

TRICEP PUSH-UPS. Supporting yourself between two benches, place your palms face down on the bench behind you, keeping your arms straight. Extend your legs straight out in front of you, propping your ankles and feet on the other bench.

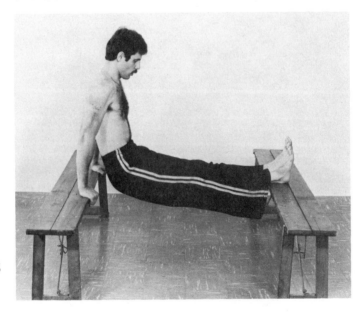

Slowly lower yourself as far as possible, then come back up to the starting position. Do 25–50 repetitions at each workout.

SIT-UPS. Sit-ups cannot be beaten for building a rock-hard midsection capable of withstanding body punches and kicks. Start with your feet under a bar, your knees up, and your hands behind your head.

Above: To keep constant tension on the abdominals, lean back only 90 percent of the way. Below: Come up twisting to the right; then repeat the series twisting to the left. Do a minimum of 50 sit-ups per training session. Eventually build up to 200 daily repetitions.

SPARRING

Through sparring you build confidence and overcome fear. It also gives you the opportunity to put into action the techniques you have drilled for endless hours. Sparring sessions are not full-contact karate matches. They are learning experiences during which your fighting strategy or style—sometimes referred to as "ring generalship"—first begins to take shape. Through sparring you quickly discover your strong and weak points, what works and what does not. Building a fighting style on your strengths and eliminating your weaknesses will make you a successful full-contact karate fighter.

Sparring Gear

When sparring, you should be fully protected, wearing safety boots, shin guards, a mouthpiece, a groin and kidney protector, a head guard, and 16-ounce boxing gloves to cushion punching techniques.

Photo by Myles Burke.

Safety Kicks

The four-ounce rubber safety kicks or boots worn during competition fit much the same way a shoe does. After applying shin and instep protectors, slip the boot on and secure the front end by putting its elastic strap around your big toe. Tie the ankle strap tightly in a bow. Then tape the boot around the instep of the foot to keep it from coming loose during competition.

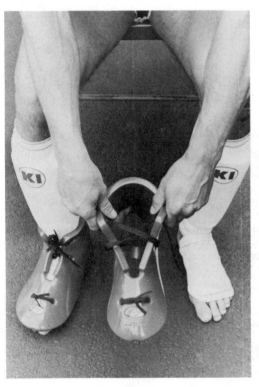 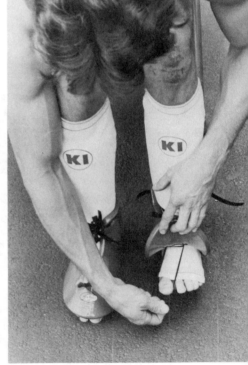

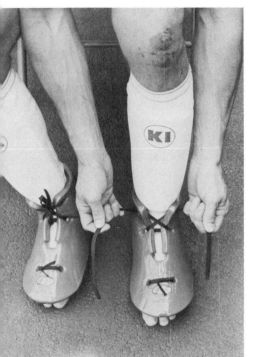

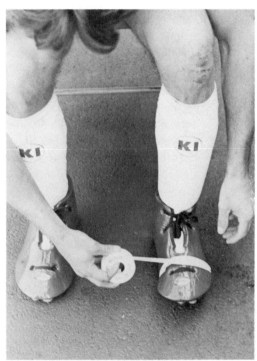

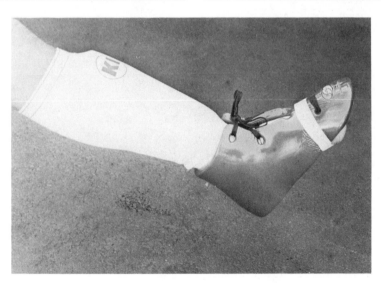

TRAINING ROUTINES

The following workout routines are designed to give you a structured guide by which to train. They incorporate the majority of exercises and techniques discussed throughout the book. The beginner's routine will prepare the amateur fighter for his first three-round bout, and the intermediate and advanced program will ready the experienced competitor for five rounds or more of full-contact competition. Stick with the routine that pertains to you for a minimum of six consecutive months and then feel free to alter or build on it along with the guidance of your trainer as your ability improves. Remember, you cannot win a world title overnight; it takes time and patience. Do not be eager to jump into a more advanced program until you have mastered the novice routine.

Beginner's Workout Routine

Running Schedule, Monday to Friday

This routine is to be done in the morning after 20 minutes of warm-up and stretching exercises.

Start by running one mile slowly every other day. Gradually increasing your distance, run three miles every day after six weeks. When running three miles, start including four 100-yard wind sprints within the run's duration. End your track work with 20 more minutes of stretching exercises to help keep the legs from becoming stiff.

Gym Training, Monday to Friday

Beginners are to perform two two-minute rounds where designated, with a one-minute rest in between.

1. *Stretching and Warm-ups:* Complete the morning's 20-minute stretching routine and warm-ups, loosening the entire body by starting with the head and working down to the ankles.

2. *Shadowboxing:* In front of a mirror, shadowbox for two rounds using only punching techniques. Concentrate on keeping

the shoulders relaxed, while snapping and retracting your punches with maximum speed.

3. *Shadowkicking:* For two rounds, again using the mirror, execute only kicking techniques, skipping in and driving your body weight behind each kick on execution.

4. *Shadowboxing and Shadowkicking:* For three rounds in the ring, move about, working from the center of the ring and off the ropes with kick-punch combinations.

5. *Sparring:* Using hands and feet, spar easily at half of maximum force with a partner for three rounds to discover and perfect techniques that work best for you.

6. *Hand Mitts:* While in the ring, work two rounds of quick one, two, punch combinations on the mitts with your opponent changing the position of the mitts in every third punching sequence.

7. *Heavy Bag:* Wearing leather bag gloves, perform two rounds of punches on the heavy bag; then do one round with kicks and punches combined.

8. *Rope Skipping:* At an easy pace, skip rope for two rounds.

9. *Musculature Exercises:* Do a minimum of 50 push-ups; a minimum of 50 tricep dips; 50–200 sit-ups; 25 medicine ball strikes to each part of the midsection, including the stomach and right and left sides.

10. *Stretching:* End with 20 minutes of light stretching to cool down and keep limber.

Photo by Tom Evans.

Intermediate and Advanced Workout Routine

Running Schedule, Monday to Saturday

This routine is to be done in the morning after 20 minutes of warm-up and stretching exercises.

Run from three to six miles six days a week with Sundays off. Include numerous sprints and some step running in your regime. This will give you explosive bursts of energy in the ring. Finish your regime with the mandatory stretching exercises. If you do not feel up to running one morning, do a very slow mile. Always keep in mind that there is a difference between fatigue and laziness.

Gym Training, Monday to Saturday

The following designated rounds are to be performed for three minutes with a minute's rest in between each round.

1. *Stretching and Warm-ups:* Do 20 minutes of stretching and warm-up exercises.

2. *Shadowboxing:* Using only punching techniques, shadowbox for three or four rounds in the ring, concentrating on footwork and defensive maneuvers.

3. *Shadowkicking:* Do three or four rounds of power kicks, working in the ring.

4. *Shadowboxing and Shadowkicking:* Do three or four rounds of kick-punch combinations.

5. *Sparring:* Do three rounds of easy sparring and two rounds of hard fighting.

6. *Hand Mitts:* Do three rounds of punching combinations in the ring with your opponent constantly moving, making it as difficult as possible for you to hit the targets.

7. *Heavy Bag:* Do three rounds of punching techniques and two rounds of kick-punch combinations.

8. *Speed Ball:* Do one round of punches to check your reflexes and timing.

9. *Rope Skipping:* Do two rounds of full-speed skipping.

10. *Musculature Exercises:* Do a minimum of 50 push-ups, a minimum of 50 tricep dips, 250–500 sit-ups, 100 medicine ball strikes to the stomach and to the right and left side of the body.

11. *Stretching:* End with 20 minutes of light stretching.

Note: This workout should be done with 100 percent effort three times a week and at an easier pace on the remaining three days. Alternate hard days with moderate days.

Photo by Tom Evans.

chapter five

stances and footwork

No matter how well your physical condition enables you to withstand blows to the body, it is worthless unless it is supported by a strong foundation to keep you from being knocked down. Hurt or not, if you are knocked to the canvas, it means the loss of precious points.

The development of strong balance and footwork comes from a fighter's stance. Although a few different types of stances are used by full-contact fighters, no other offers better protection, balance, and mobility for executing effective kicking and punching techniques than the following.

STANCE TECHNIQUE

The stance is an upright posture that is assumed by placing your feet slightly farther than shoulder width apart with the rear leg approximately one foot off to the side. If you are right-handed, your left foot is forward; if you are a southpaw (left-handed), your right foot is forward. The front foot is flat on the ground with the rear foot on the ball, keeping the heel approximately three inches off the ground. With the rear foot in this position you will have quicker mobility and faster kick execution. The knees are always bent slightly for flexibility with your weight distributed evenly on both legs.

With your legs positioned properly and your fists held high, turn your torso sideways with your lead shoulder facing your opponent. By turning you protect your midsection and give your jab greater reach.

With the torso turned, keep your face squarely toward your opponent and your chin tucked into your chest for protection. Keep your eyes on your opponent, looking into his chest, which will enable you to see any movement he may make with either his hands or his feet.

Now lean your torso forward two inches at the waist, not at the shoulders, to help cover and tighten the abdominal muscles. Besides protecting the body, tilting forward brings you closer to your opponent, which will give you greater power, reach, accuracy, and leverage in your punching techniques. Also, tilting your head forward a little draws your opponent unconsciously toward you as if to sucker him into what he believes is an easy-to-hit head target. In reality you are setting him up by getting him to attack so you can counter.

These little-known upper body maneuvers are much more effective than standing straight up all the time. A fighter who keeps his back straight and his head up often tends to back away from punches instead of holding his ground and countering. Avoid this mistake at all costs.

FOOTWORK

There are three purposes of footwork: (1) to move in on your opponent, (2) to move away from your opponent, and (3) to set up your opponent.

A

B

C

All three must be done as quickly as possible and with the least amount of detection by your opponent. Whether you are amateur or pro, the formula for effective footwork basically is as follows: when moving forward, the front foot moves first; when moving back, the back foot moves first; when moving to the right side, the right foot moves first; and when going to the left, the left foot moves first.

When performing these maneuvers, your body should stay stable, with your feet leaving the ground as seldom as possible to keep your balance strong. Avoid bouncing and jumping from stance to stance; this only leaves you more vulnerable to counterattacks by your opponent if he catches you in between stances. Remember, there is very little margin for error in the fast-paced sport of full-contact fighting; a minor mistake can mean an instant knockout.

Another point to be aware of is that, whenever you are maneuvering, you should be able to kick, punch, and defend properly. If not, you are off balance and must correct your stance immediately.

Photo by Myles Burke.

POSITIONING

When you are in the ring, there is an excellent guide you can use to establish your position against your opponent and your point of direction: stand with your lead leg focused in between your opponent's legs, aiming your front foot at your opponent's groin. This will keep you in range of your opponent's vital areas and enable you to follow his movements, whether he moves to the right, left, front, or back.

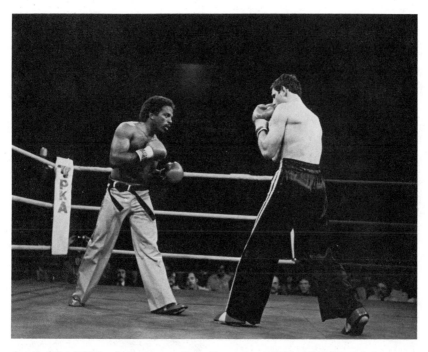

April 25, 1981, facing number 2 ranked PKA Middleweight contender Rodney Batiste, I positioned myself so my lead leg was lined up in between his legs, enabling me to control the ring and have access to all targets. I went on to win a 12-round decision over Batiste. Photo by Tom Evans.

Most fighters make the mistake of placing their front leg directly in front of their opponent's lead leg, which automatically limits their mobility to strike the full range of their opponent's midsection and destroys their ability to control the ring and cut off their adversary's movements.

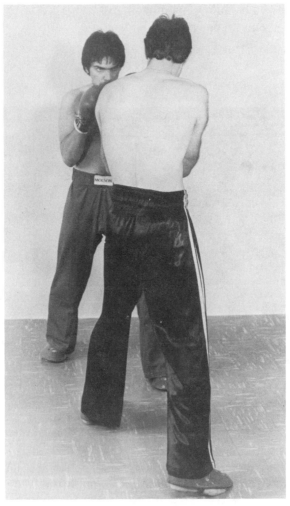

Stance positioning, rear view.

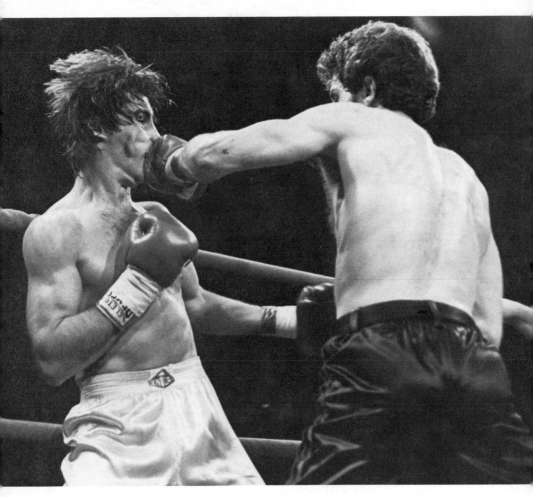

Photo by Tom Evans.

chapter six

punching techniques

The punching skills used in full-contact karate are exactly the same as those used in boxing. Any previous boxing training you have will definitely be a bonus in learning full-contact karate. After mastering the following five basic punches, the trick is to coordinate them successfully with your kicking techniques, which will be discussed thoroughly in Chapter 9.

For your hand techniques to score, the following points must be applied to the execution of them:

1. For speed and accuracy, execute your punches directly from the guard position, without winding up, to avoid giving your movement away.

2. After completing a punch, immediately retract your hand to the guard position.

3. Keep your shoulders and arms loose when punching; tighten the body only when your punch makes contact.

4. Although you will be unable to kick when you are down in a crouch position, delivering punches to the body, get in the habit of coming up out of the crouch executing a kick.

5. Concentrate on putting your body behind each punch for maximum power.

JAB TO THE HEAD

The jab is used mainly to set up your opponent for combinations and to keep him at bay because of its long reach. It is also used to snap out at your opponent to judge your distance, which will give you an idea of how much ground you must cover when going in.

Below, left: Ready position. Below, right: Begin striking with your lead hand from the guard position to avoid telegraphing your movement.

Left: Complete the jab by extending your arm and sharply turning your fist in a corkscrew motion. The turn of the fist adds impact and helps raise your shoulder to protect your chin from counterstrikes. At all times, concentrate on keeping your chin in toward your shoulder as shown. Below, left: Jab, front view. Below, right: The jab, applied to the face.

JAB TO THE BODY. Ready position.

When striking low to the midsection, never stand straight up and punch down. Always drop your body weight straight down, keeping your shoulders level and your head up.

78

Lean forward on the front leg, completing the jab to the midsection.

The jab, applied to the midsection.

RIGHT CROSS TO THE FACE

The right cross is a very good knockout punch that usually follows a left jab lead.

Below, left: Ready position. Below, right: Striking with the back hand, turn your hip and body into the punch as you begin to strike.

Complete the punch by completely extending your arm and twisting your fist. Keep the face well protected by the shoulder of the punching arm and keep the body covered with the nonpunching arm.

The right cross, applied to the face.

RIGHT CROSS TO THE BODY.
Ready position.

Begin by turning your hip into the
punch as you start to strike, dropping your body weight down while
keeping the shoulders level.

82

Complete the punch by extending your arm and twisting your fist. Again, note the good head and body protection achieved by keeping the chin in and the opposite hand held high.

The right cross, applied to the mid-section.

HOOK PUNCH TO THE FACE

A close-in fighting technique, the hook punch is used to come around your opponent's guard. Its circular motion makes it hard to see, let alone defend against.

Below, left: Ready position. Below, right: Arc your lead hand around coming from the outside in.

Complete the punch by turning your body sharply as you hook into the side of the head. Ninety percent of this punch's power is created by putting your body's motion behind it.

The hook punch, applied to the face. Photo by Tom Evans.

HOOK PUNCH TO THE BODY. Ready position.

Drop down and lean forward with your hip facing straight at your opponent.

86

As in the hook to the head, turn your body sharply with the punch.

The hook punch, applied to the body.

OVERHAND RIGHT

This is similar to the right cross, but instead of being thrown on a straight line to the target, it is looped over your opponent's guard, striking his head.

Ready position.

Above: Begin turning your hips, arching the punch over your opponent's guard. Below: Complete the punch by striking down into the jaw or temple.

UPPERCUT TO THE JAW

Because of its lack of extension, the uppercut is used for tight situations, such as when you are on the ropes or in a clinch.

Above, left: Ready position. Above, right: Turning your body directly at your opponent, drop down slightly, bringing your rear hand low as you move.

Follow through by driving the punch straight up under the jaw, pushing off from your knees.

The uppercut, applied to the jaw. Photo by Tom Evans.

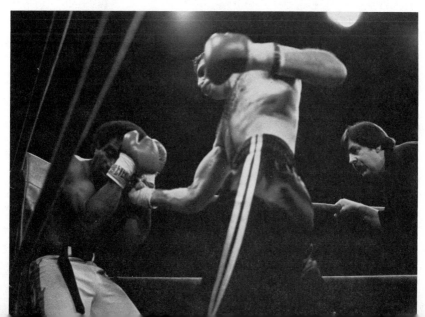

A   **B**

UPPERCUT TO THE BODY. **(A)** Ready position. **(B)** Drop low and
into your opponent **(C)**, keeping your hips at an angle. **(D)** The
uppercut, applied to the body. Photo by Myles Burke.

92

C

D

Knocking out Jarvis Gardner in the sixth round with a lead leg roundhouse kick to the head, January 1982 in Montreal, Canada. Photo by Myles Burke.

chapter seven

kicking techniques

INTRODUCTION TO KICKS

The excitement that full-contact karate generates among its many fans can most often be attributed to the spectacular kicking techniques executed during a match. With each fighter required to throw a minimum of eight kicks per two-minute round, and the average more often being 15 kicks per round, the action becomes nonstop.

The main purpose of kicking is to intimidate, punish, and keep your opponent at bay. Although kicks are more powerful than punches, contrary to popular belief, they only account for 25 percent of all knockouts. This is due to the fact that kicks are harder to develop than punches, as well as easier to avoid, less accurate, and more demanding on one's stamina, which causes them to decrease in effectiveness rather rapidly.

Photo by Russo.

A fighter's kicking ability during a match will quickly separate the strong fighters from the weak and will usually determine the outcome of a bout. Hard kick training and intensive leg conditioning exercises, such as those mentioned earlier, are the only route to survival and to kicking with damaging force during all scheduled rounds.

Full-contact karate has quite a stable of fancy kickers who thrive on executing a number of flashy kicks such as spinning, flying, and multiple-kicking with the same leg during their bouts. Many of these flashy kicks look impressive, but more often than not they lack the accuracy and power to wear down or knock out your opponent. *Stay away from these kicks;* they leave you off balance and more vulnerable to a counterstrike.

The seven basic full-contact kicks that have brought me the world title and are sure to bring you victory are the lead leg front kick, the rear leg front kick, the side kick, the lead leg roundhouse kick, the rear leg roundhouse kick, the hook kick, and the ax kick.

For any of these kicks to generate their full force on impact, the following points must be applied.

96

KICKING EXECUTION

More important than the actual extension of the leg when kicking is the initial triggering of the kicking leg or positioning of it into what is commonly referred to as the chamber. This is done by bringing the kicking leg knee up high into the chest just prior to kicking. The initial chamber movement gives you greater thrusting power, speed, and mobility and acts as a guard to protect the midsection against counterstrikes. When the knee is high the supporting leg should be kept bent slightly for balance and flexibility, with your guard held protectively.

Prior to the kick's execution the body should be semirelaxed for greater speed, and when striking you should drive your body weight behind the kick, tightening all your muscles on impact. Keep the foot in the proper striking position to avoid unnecessary injuries. These points must also be applied when practicing kicks on training equipment.

As part of my fight strategy during a match I often use the power of my kicks to intimidate and scare my opponent by purposely blasting rear leg roundhouse kicks directly into his guard. Although they do not score, the contact made numbs the arms, thus weakening his defense and punching power.

Occasional power kicks to your opponent's guard will numb his arms and weaken his defense. Photo by Tom Evans.

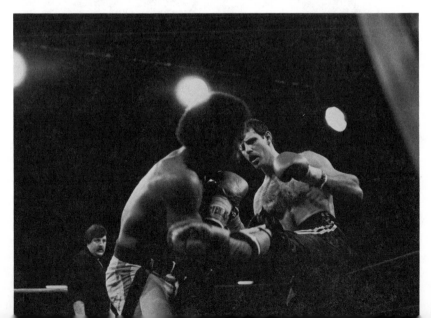

To become as adept as possible in your kicking ability, practice with each leg equally when training.

In competition, execute 80 percent of your kicks to the midsection, going high to the head only when your opponent has been weakened and made vulnerable. Kicks to the midsection are faster and stronger than head kicks because of the shorter distance they have to travel. They also enable you to regain your balance more quickly.

One last point you must constantly be aware of is to retract your kicking leg and set it down in a position that will give you good balance for a strong offensive or defensive follow-up technique.

FOOT POSITIONS

Kicks will be unable to deliver 100 percent of their destructive

BALL OF FOOT. Keep your foot straight and your toes pulled back tightly, making contact with the ball or padded area. This position is used exclusively when executing front kicks.

force unless the foot is in the proper position. Proper foot positions absorb the shock of impact, preventing injuries such as broken toes and sprained ankles. The four foot positions of full-contact karate kicking follow.

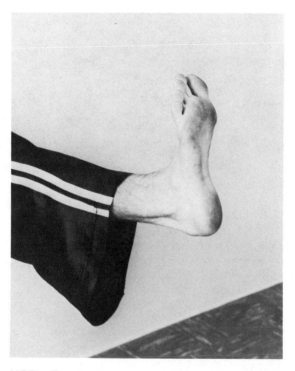

HEEL. The heel position is formed by pulling your foot straight back to accentuate the heel. Used less often than the ball of the foot, it is associated with straight-line foot kicks.

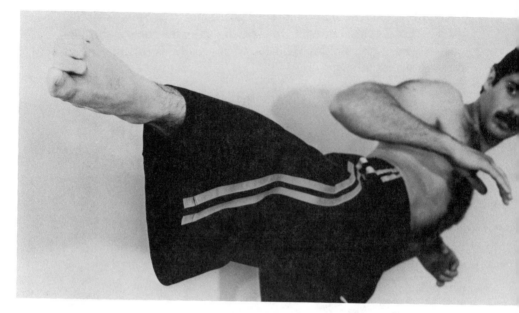

INSTEP AND SHIN. For front and rear leg roundhouse kicks to the ribs, kidneys, midsection, and head, form the instep by curling the toes down and striking with the top of the foot. When your opponent is at a close distance your foot position remains the same, but contact is made with the shin.

BLADE. Position your foot by pushing your heel out and pulling your toes in toward you to bring out the edge and heel of the foot for striking. The blade is used with side and hook kicks.

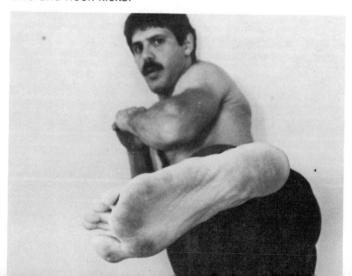

LEAD LEG FRONT KICK

This kick is used most often in full-contact karate because of its quickness and accuracy, and because it allows you to gauge your opponent's distance.

Above, left: Ready position. Above, right: Skipping forward the approximate distance, your feet apart in your ready stance, quickly thrust your knee high into your chest.

Above, left: Kick out into the midsection. Above, right: The kick follows through to the head area. Contact is made with the ball of the foot. *Note:* As with all kicks, put your body weight behind the kick for ultimate force.

REAR LEG FRONT KICK. Above, left: Guard position. Above, right: Raise your rear leg into the chest to protect the midsection, keeping your guard up and your elbows tight in toward your rib cage.

Thrust your kicking leg into your opponent's solar plexus, making contact with the ball of the foot.

The rear leg front kick, applied to the midsection. Photo by Tom Evans.

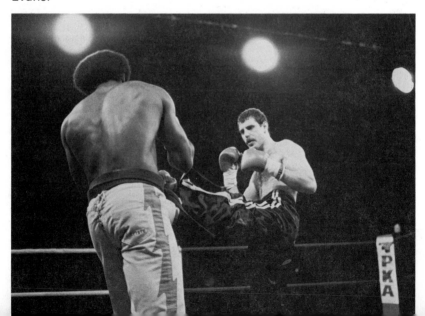

When kicking to the head with a front kick, try to connect under your opponent's jaw. Lean back slightly for greater extension.

The front kick, applied to the jaw. Photo by Myles Burke.

LEAD LEG ROUNDHOUSE KICK

This kick is faster but not quite as powerful as the rear leg roundhouse kick. The lead leg roundhouse kick is used mainly as a defensive technique to kick underneath your opponent's punching attack. It is ideal for countering a right cross or a jab to the head.

Above, left: Ready position. Above, right: Skipping forward or back, depending on the situation, raise your front leg high into the chamber.

Thrust the kick into the opponent's midsection by turning your supporting foot and hip into the kick so that your shoulders end up sideways to your opponent. Contact is made with the instep or shin.

The lead leg roundhouse is also delivered to the head when countering body punches.

REAR LEG ROUNDHOUSE KICK

This is full-contact's most destructive kick because of the great power fighters can generate from its kicking motion.

Above, left: Ready position. Above, right: At the same time, pivot your supporting foot and bring your rear leg up with its knee pointing at your opponent.

Above, left: Turning your hip sharply, drive your leg into the opponent's midsection, making contact with the instep or shin, depending on the distance between you and your opponent. Above, right: The rear leg roundhouse kick, applied to the midsection.

Above, left: Repeating the first two steps, execute a roundhouse to the head. Above, right: The rear leg roundhouse, applied to the head.

SIDE KICK

The side kick is delivered with the lead leg. It is usually used as a defensive weapon because of the great extension it offers.

Ready position.

Above, left: With your body perpendicular (sideways) to your opponent, raise your lead leg into the chamber, keeping the foot in the blade position. Above, right: Keeping your guard tight in toward your body, turn your hip and supporting foot 45 degrees in the opposite direction of the kick, at the same time thrusting your leg out to the opponent's midsection.

The side kick, applied to the ribs.

The side kick, applied to the head.

HOOK KICK

Although a very powerful kick, the hook kick is used least in competition because it is a bit slower to execute and control than the front, side, and roundhouse kicks. It should still be developed because it does have knockout power.

Below, left: Guard position. Below, right: Slide forward, bringing your lead leg up high as if ready to throw a side kick, keeping your foot in the blade position.

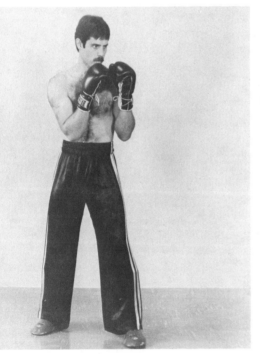 

Shoot your leg out to the side of your opponent, then quickly whip your foot into his head,
making contact with the heel.

Arc of the kick completed.

The hook kick, applied to the head.

AX KICK

A very intimidating and hard-to-block kicking technique I use is the little-known ax kick. This kick is used to punish your opponent's arms to create openings in his defense.

Above: Ready position. Below: Raise your lead leg as if attempting a front kick.

Above: Thrust your leg straight up over your opponent's guard. Below: With the toes pulled back, drive your leg straight down on your opponent's guard making contact with the heel.

Above: Push his arms down. Below: Then follow through by setting your kicking leg forward and following with a punch to the exposed face area.

JUMP KICKS

To add power to certain kicks it's occasionally effective to jump into them. This type of technique should be used only when your opponent has been dazed or is incapable of defending effectively, because an alert opponent can avoid these kicks more easily than kicks delivered from a stationary position. Using the front or roundhouse kick, simply jump up and toward your target, slamming your entire body weight behind the action.

Full-contact karate jump kicks are not be to be confused with the high-flying traditional karate kicks in which practitioners kick for maximum height. The high-flying kicks leave you in too dangerous a position for full-contact, where someone is waiting to take your head off when you land.

Jump front kick.

Jump rear leg roundhouse kick.

Blocking and jamming an attempted side kick by light heavyweight Kerry Roop, April 19, 1979. Photo by Armand Legault.

chapter eight

developing a
stonewall defense

The top fighters in full-contact karate and boxing are the ones with the fewest scars. They have the ability to defeat their opponents while getting hit very little in the process. This comes from a very intelligent defensive fighting strategy. Never take the tough guy attitude of "I'll take a punch to give one"; this is pure stupidity and will cut your fight career short.

As stated earlier in the book, a protective defense is one of the main areas in which full-contact karate fighters are dangerously lacking. This comes from assuming incorrect guard positions and poor defensive techniques. In this chapter we will thoroughly discuss the defensive maneuvers so important to a fighter's survival, starting with basic guards to blocking, parrying, and slipping. Remember, a fighter cannot begin to have a good offense until he has first mastered an effective defense.

GUARDS AND BLOCKING TECHNIQUES

A good guard is one that is made by keeping the hands close together at chin height with the elbows held in tight to the rib cage. The upper torso should be turned sideways, with the lead shoulder pointing at your opponent to protect your midsection. When you are in this position, your opponent will have a difficult time penetrating your defense, while you should be able to block 90 percent of his blows by taking the majority of them on the gloves and arms.

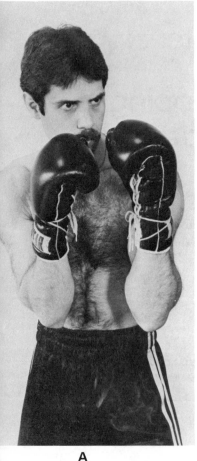

A **B** **C**

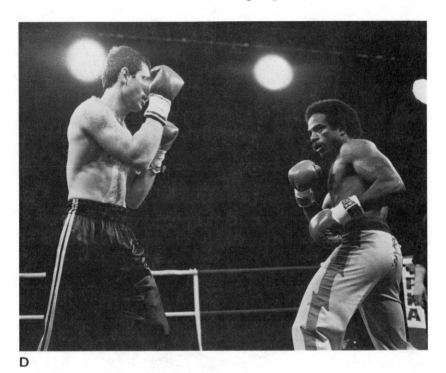

D

(A) PROPER GUARD. **(B)** IMPROPER GUARDS. A common mistake is to drop the lead arm, leaving the entire midsection and head exposed. It also makes it hard to execute quick jabs without your punch being telegraphed. **(C)** As dangerous as leaving one hand low is to fight with both hands down below chin level. The head is left fully unprotected, and your punching power is weakened because of poor leverage. **(D)** A contrast in styles. My opponent makes the mistake of leaving his lead hand dangerously low, thus exposing his entire head area. Photo by Tom Evans.

PARRYING

Parrying is used to deflect your opponent's punch, knocking him off balance, leaving him vulnerable to a counterstrike.

BLOCKING THE JAB. Keeping your guard high, stop your opponent's jab simply by bringing your gloves together, catching the strike in the palms.

UPPERCUT BLOCK. As your opponent attempts an uppercut to the jaw, twist your shoulder, blocking the punch with your forearm.

BODY PUNCH BLOCK. Block punches to the body by turning your guard into the strike, blocking with your forearm.

BLOCKING A ROUNDHOUSE KICK TO THE MIDSECTION. If unable to evade a kick, hold your ground, keeping your guard in place, blocking with your forearm. Photo by Tom Evans.

BLOCKING A ROUNDHOUSE KICK TO THE HEAD. Raise your hand to catch the force of the kick on your glove. Photo by Tom Evans.

SPINNING BACK KICK BLOCK. As your opponent spins and throws a straight leg back kick to the head, move in, jamming and catching the kick with your arms before your opponent can extend his leg full-force. This is not an easy kick to counter because you usually end up out of striking reach.

SIDE KICK BLOCK. Protect your midsection from this powerful kick by pulling your arms tightly together and tensing your body on impact.

129

KNEE AND ARM BLOCK. Above, left: To add to the effectiveness of your handheld guards, raise your lead leg knee to your elbow to block a rear leg roundhouse kick to the body. Above, right: With your opponent balanced on only one leg, you are now in an excellent position to step forward and counter with a jab to the face.

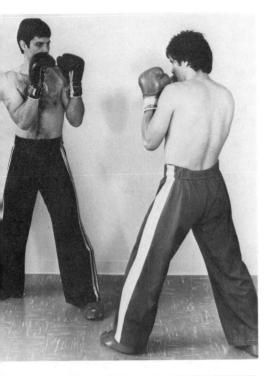

Left: Ready position. Below, left: As your opponent starts his jab, turn your body, bringing your rear hand forward. Below, right: With your rear hand, redirect your opponent's punch by slapping it to the side. Your opponent is now open to various counterattacks.

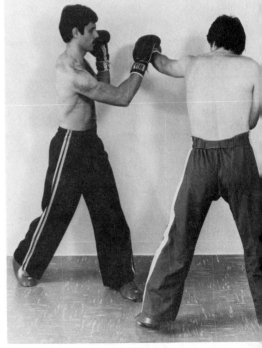

SLIPPING

Slipping is totally avoiding your opponent's kick or punch but not backing away from the attack to a point at which you cannot execute a counterstrike. To slip is to hold your ground and sway down, sideways, and back out of the direct line of your opponent's offensive or defensive attack. It is perfected by sparring in the ring for two or three rounds and having your partner attack you with a variety of techniques, which you slip and counter to develop your reflexes. In the beginning you may be grazed by your opponent, which should be no problem as long as he is unable to connect solidly.

The following slipping motion must be done quickly and continuously without stopping. Remember to keep your stance solid, your guard up, your shoulders level, and your eyes on your opponent's chest area. Although the initial movement is to the right in the photos, you can also do the maneuver by starting on the left.

A

B

(A) Ready position. **(B)** Begin slipping punches by swaying to the right. **(C)** Circling down and forward. **(D)** Continue by moving to the left side with the guard covering at all times. **(E)** Finish by rotating back to the starting position.

E

SLIPPING A JAB TO THE FACE.
Above, left: Ready position. Above,
right: As your opponent begins his
left-handed jab to the face, start
slipping to the left. Right: Avoid the
punch and counter with an overhand right to the jaw.

134

SLIPPING A HEAD PUNCH COUN-
TER TO THE BODY. Above, left:
Ready position. Above, right: Holding your ground, begin to slip to
your right as your opponent starts
throwing a left jab to your head.
Right: Complete your slip and counter by dropping low, executing a
left-hand jab to the midsection.

SLIPPING A RIGHT CROSS. Left: Ready position. Below, left: When the right cross is thrown, slip down and to the right. Below, right: Counter with a right-hand uppercut to the solar plexus.

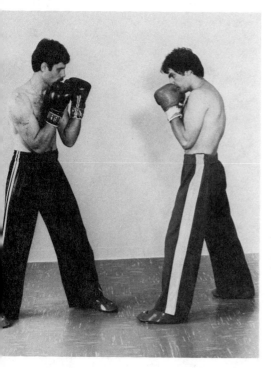

HOOK PUNCH SLIP. Above, left: Ready position. Above, right: When a close-in technique like the right-hand hook is thrown to the head, drop under the punch. Right: Counter with a left hook to the body.

A   B

FRONT KICK SLIP. (A) Ready position. (B) As your attacker begins his front kick, hold your ground and begin leaning back. (C) Keep 80 percent of your weight on the rear leg as you lean away from the kick's reach. (D) As your opponent sets his kicking leg down, lean forward into him in a good countering position. (E) Counter with a left jab to the face.

C

D

E

SIDE KICK SLIP. Ready position.

Begin to slip and lean to the outside of your opponent
as he begins his side kick.

Again, hold your ground as the kick goes by.

Lean back into your opponent as he sets his leg down, executing a right cross to his head.

JAMMING

Jamming is used to move in on your opponent in the midst of his attack, catching him off balance. It takes sharp reflexes and perfect timing to pull it off.

FRONT KICK JAMMING TECHNIQUE. **(A)** Ready position. **(B)** As the knee is raised to kick, lean forward with your arms in tight, covering your midsection. **(C)** With the attempted kick cut off and powerless, counter with a right cross to the jaw.

A

B

C

DEFENSIVE LEG TECHNIQUES

You will find that using the legs as defensive weapons will make up 40 percent of your blocking techniques. A kick offers twice the reach of a punch, making kicks excellent for stopping your opponent in midattack and keeping him out of striking range.

FRONT LEG JAB. **(A)** Ready position. **(B)** As your opponent begins a roundhouse kick, raise your lead leg. **(C)** Skip in and push hard into your opponent's midsection or face, knocking him back off balance. The foot jab is not a knockout kick but is great for frustrating your opponent's offensive attempts. Due to the front leg kick's speed, this kick scores frequently when used as a jabbing technique.

A

144

B

C

145

A

B

146

DEFENSIVE FRONT KICK. **(A)** Ready position. **(B)** Sensing your opponent's punch, raise your lead leg. **(C)** Counter with a front kick to the solar plexus or face. Notice the reach advantage you have over your opponent.

C

SIDE KICK COUNTER. **(A)** Ready position. **(B)** Holding your ground, bring your front leg into the chamber. **(C)** Throw a side kick to the ribs, making contact with the blade of your foot.

B

C

ROUNDHOUSE KICK COUNTER. **(A)** Ready position. **(B)** As your opponent attempts a right cross to the face, slip the punch by going to the left, readying your right leg. **(C)** Complete a roundhouse kick to the side of head.

A

B

C

Setting a world PKA record by knocking out Mark Zacharatos in 21 seconds of the first round in a May 1982 title defense held in Windsor, Canada. A combination roundhouse kick to the ribs, followed by a left hook and an overhand right to the head did the job. PKA referee Jay T. Will counts Zacharatos out.

chapter nine

knockout combinations

In full-contact karate a combination is two or more techniques thrown in succession, and it can include two punches, two kicks, or, more often, punches and kicks combined. The main purpose of offensive and defensive combinations is to strike your opponent with a flurry of techniques without giving him time to react effectively.

To develop winning combinations you must begin by perfecting a series of basic movements that easily follow each other, such as a left jab, right cross, front kick sequence. This can easily be repeated in reverse by executing the front kick first, then following with a right cross and left jab. In full-contact karate the rule of thumb is that, when you start a combination with a punch, you follow with a kick; when starting with a kick, you follow with a punch.

As your ability improves, build on your combinations, putting together a variety of techniques that bring out your strong points as a fighter. Combinations that are fluid in sequence give you better balance, speed, and accuracy than techniques that are awkward in succession.

The first technique of a combination is the most important because it sets up your opponent. If your initial attack dazes your opponent or brings down his guard, the techniques to follow are sure to score and do damage. Execute your first technique explosively and with good timing, catching your opponent at his weakest point.

Always begin combinations with the lead leg or hand, because

The first technique of a combination should stun your opponent, leaving him open for the techniques that follow. Photo by Myles Burke.

Mix up your combinations so they confuse and frustrate your opponent. Photo by Tom Evans.

they are closer to your opponent, thus giving you greater reach and speed than when beginning with the rear hand or foot. Since speed is of the essence in pulling off your combinations, always begin your next technique as the prior one is being retracted.

To confuse your opponent, combinations should consist of a variety of head and body shots. For example, a kick to the body is good to bring an opponent's guard down as you follow with a punch or another kick to the head. Aiming all your techniques at one target makes them predictable and easy to evade.

An important point to realize when attempting combinations is the distance between you and your opponent. At all times each technique in your series should be able to make hard contact with your opponent. A simple rule for developing proper distancing is to attack with combinations only when contact with your opponent can be made by moving forward or back the same distance that your feet are spread apart.

Though the following photos show each technique of a combination delivered with proper form and accuracy, this is not always going to happen in a true fight situation. When your opponent is

155

attacked he certainly is not going to be standing in one spot waiting for you to beat on him. Due to the fact that he will be moving unpredictably, you must apply the proper footwork to your combinations, instinctively compensating for any front, back, or side movement your opponent may make.

OFFENSIVE COMBINATIONS

When on the attack, always try to initiate the first technique of your combination when your opponent is at his weakest.

Weaknesses occur when a fighter shifts from stance to stance, drops his guard, loses concentration for a moment, or is confused by a feinting technique.

The only way to learn to read and take advantage of these weaknesses effectively is through extensive sparring sessions.

FRONT KICK, JAB, OVERHAND RIGHT. Ready position.

Keeping your guard high, bring your lead leg up.

Execute a front kick to the midsection.

Above: As your opponent drops his hands, step into him with a left jab to the nose. Right: Turn your body, delivering an overhand right to the head.

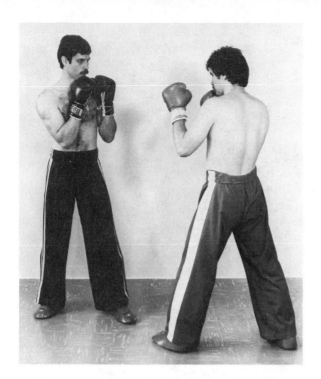

HOOK KICK, RIGHT CROSS, JAB.
Above: Ready position. Right: Skip
at your opponent, bringing your
front leg up with the foot in the
blade position.

A

(A) Hook into your opponent's head, striking his temple with your heel. (B) With your opponent dazed, follow with a right cross to the ribs. (C) End with a left jab to the nose.

B

C

SIDE KICK, RIGHT UPPERCUT, LEFT HOOK. Ready position.

Skip in, triggering your lead leg.

Do a side kick to the ribs.

Your opponent buckles forward.

You then shoot a right uppercut to the jaw.

Finish with a left hook to the head.

JAB, RIGHT CROSS, ROUNDHOUSE, FRONT KICK.
Ready position.

Execute a piercing left jab to the opponent's nose.

Follow with a right cross to the jaw.

With your opponent's guard broken, raise your rear leg.

Do a roundhouse to the ribs.

Set the kick down, bringing your opposite leg up.

Finish with a rear leg front kick to the solar plexus.

Foot Sweep, Right Cross

Though I seldom use sweeping techniques, they are legal and are good for knocking your opponent off balance.

Ready position.

A

(A) Begin the sweep by swinging your rear leg around. (B) With your instep, knock your opponent's leg out from under him, hitting him above the ankle. (C) Follow with a right cross to the jaw.

170

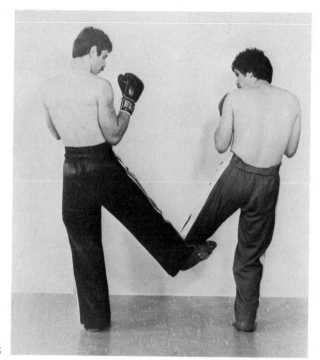

B

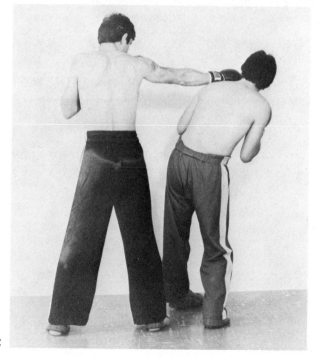

C

171

Front Kick, Uppercut, Left Hook, Right Cross, Left Hook, Roundhouse Kick to Ribs, Two Roundhouse Kicks to Head

The following combination is a typical one I would use when trapping my opponent against the ropes. The entire sequence would be executed in a matter of seconds.

A

(A) Ready position. **(B)** With the opponent driven to the ropes, ready a front kick to the opponent's open midsection. **(C)** Score a front kick.

B

C

Follow with a right-hand uppercut to the jaw.

Come across with a left hook.

Do a right cross to the jaw.

Follow with a left hook to the body.

A

(A) Then do a rear leg roundhouse kick to the ribs. **(B)** Follow with another roundhouse to the head. **(C)** End with a rear leg jump roundhouse kick to the head.

B

C

177

DEFENSIVE COMBINATIONS

Successful defensive fighting in full-contact karate requires excellent timing and courage. The only way to defend and counter the onslaught of your opponent's kicks and punches is by holding your ground and staying within powerful striking range.

The courage to hold your ground in the ring will develop by perfecting the basic defensive guards and slipping maneuvers explained in Chapter 8.

Ready position.

It's important to develop your defensive counters and timing to the point where you can detect and often sense your opponent's offensive maneuvers even before he begins them. Therefore, I suggest you train by sparring strictly defensively for numerous rounds against an aggressive offensive fighter.

Defending against a Foot Sweep

Just as important as knowing how to execute a foot sweep is knowing how to defend against one.

As your leg is struck, keep its momentum going.

Bring your leg up, ready to kick.

Before your opponent can start his counter technique, execute a defensive side kick to the rib cage.

FRONT KICK, ROUNDHOUSE. Ready position.

Using your legs, reach to your advantage; ready a front leg kick as your opponent begins to jab.

181

A

B

182

C

(A) Kick to the solar plexus. (B) Set the kick down and trigger the opposite leg for a roundhouse kick. (C) Complete the kick by striking to the opponent's head.

UPPERCUT, HOOK PUNCH, FRONT KICK. Ready position.

Slip to the right, avoiding a jab to the head.

Follow with a right uppercut to the jaw.

Continue with a left hook.

With your opponent defenseless, begin a front kick.

Complete the front kick to the face.

Sidestep, Overhand Right, Counter

During a match it is quite common for fighters to try spinning kicks and punches. These are gambles and should never be attempted because you momentarily lose sight of your opponent, leaving yourself open for counterstrikes, as the following photos show.

Left: Ready position. Below, left: As your opponent begins turning to execute a spinning back kick, sidestep to your left, avoiding the kick's line of fire. Below, right: Slide in on your opponent and quickly counter with an overhand right to the temple.

SPINNING BACK FIST COUN-
TER. Ready position.

Hold your ground as your opponent begins his spin.

188

Raise your gloves to block the head strike.

Counter with a short left uppercut to the ribs.

189

ROUNDHOUSE KICK, BLOCK, DOUBLE PUNCH COUNTER. **(A)** Ready position. **(B)** Stay firm as your opponent readies a back leg roundhouse kick to the body. **(C)** Block his kick with your guard. **(D)** Then counter with a left hook to the face. **(E)** Follow with a right cross to the jaw.

A

B

C

D

E

191

DEFENDING ON THE ROPES

If caught on the ropes, use your kicks to keep your opponent off you until you can escape.

Photo by Myles Burke.

Use the ropes to your advantage by leaning against them with your front leg up.

Kick out at your opponent's midsection.

If your opponent keeps coming, bounce off the ropes, sidestepping his assault.

Counter his punch with a left hook to the jaw.

CLINCHING

A mistake fighters make when clinching is to struggle fiercely with their opponent in an effort to punch him in the body and head. This is a waste of time and energy because your arms are not free enough to land effective blows. The proper way to react when clinching is to stay relaxed to conserve energy and to hold your opponent's arms around the elbows to keep him from punching. Always keep your head down on his shoulder with the chin tucked in to avoid being head butted. The advantage clinching offers is that it gives a hurt fighter a moment's rest.

Photo by Tom Evans.

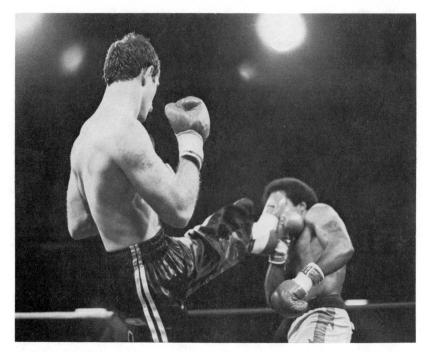

Photo by Tom Evans.

chapter ten

winning fight strategy

As explained in Chapter 4, your fight strategy and style begin to take shape in sparring sessions. Often a student will attempt to adopt the style of another fighter, which is a mistake because no two fighters are alike in their approach to the sport. Even though fighters sometimes look similar in posture and technique, they are quite different because of physical abilities and mental attitudes. It is best to constantly look into yourself for development because successful fight strategy must be an ongoing process, using your own judgment along with the recommendations of your coach as ways of improving your fight game.

My personal strategy is to control the ring by relentlessly pursuing and pressuring my opponent, giving him little time to think and respond effectively. Through severe training and total

Never in retreat, I always pressure my opponents, causing them to make costly mistakes. This ring strategy has brought me early round knockouts over my opponents and the World title. Photo by Tom Evans.

dedication, this plan of wearing down my opponent has worked successfully for me and is responsible for the fact that 90 percent of my wins have been early round knockouts.

Though I am fortunate to end most of my matches quickly, I would much rather fight the distance and win by a decision over my opponent. This is because going the distance puts me to the test, calling on all my capabilities as a fighter to show superior endurance, technique, strategy, determination, and intelligence over my opponent. For me there is no greater feeling of accomplishment than to be judged the winner after having fought 12 hard rounds in the full-contact karate arena against a courageous opponent.

Experience has shown the following 25 points to be the most important in developing a full-contact karate fighter's ring strategy. Study them and apply them to your training.

STRATEGY POINTERS

1. Your best beginning strategy in a bout is to fight a defensive fight with a strong offensive mental attitude. This means leaving deceptive openings, tempting your opponent to take chances, and then taking advantage of it when he exposes a weakness.

2. A successful fighter is a thinking fighter, who wins with a sharp mind capable of making the right decisions in a split second. This skill is more important than just using your physical abilities to slug it out. A smart fighter can outmaneuver a slugger, wearing him down and picking him off at will. Fight with your brains, not your brawn.

3. If a technique works, keep doing it until your opponent picks up on it.

4. Use a variety of techniques. If your opponent protects his head well, avoid the head and go to the body.

After knocking your opponent down or out you will be directed to a neutral corner by the referee. Photo by Tom Evans.

5. Learn to fight from the center of the ring, keeping control of your opponent and maneuvering him where you want him, such as into the corner or against the ropes.

6. When caught against the ropes or in a corner, use your front leg to keep your opponent off you. Escape the ropes by slipping to the sides. When in a corner, the only escape is straight ahead; fight your way out again by using your front kick to the midsection.

7. No matter how superior you may be to your opponent, never carry a fight longer than it takes to achieve victory. Trying to please the audience by keeping the fight going for more rounds could mean disaster because you are increasing the chances that your opponent will slip in a lucky punch that could knock you out.

8. If you see your opponent tiring, turn on the pressure, which will burn him out more quickly.

9. Never get involved with judging or decisions. If you feel bad calls are being made, tell your trainer and have him take care of it.

10. Listen carefully to your cornermen in between rounds. Your coach is capable of seeing mistakes and openings in your opponent that you may fail to recognize. Apply his advice and evaluate the results. If it works, fine; if not, seek another route.

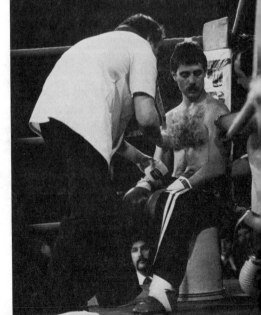

Good cornermen are a must for reviving and encouraging you between rounds.

200

A good fight strategy is to hold your ground consistently and remain within countering distance of your opponent's attack. Photo by Myles Burke.

11. Since you must execute eight kicks per round, pay attention to the kick counter near your corner. He will hold up cards showing the amount of kicks you have thrown. It is wise to get your kicks in within the first half of the round when your stamina is at its strongest.

12. Do not rush in wildly at your opponent; pace yourself, attacking only when the possibility of scoring is good.

13. When in trouble, avoid mixing it up with your opponent. Keep him at bay with jabs and kicks until you can clear your head.

14. Apply faking techniques throughout your fight to check your opponent's reaction and to upset his defense.

15. Never fight your opponent's fight; always stick to your major strategy.

16. If your opponent tries taking cheap shots, never retaliate by doing the same because you may end up being penalized. The referee will eventually catch the rule-breaking fighter.

17. If possible, observe videotapes of fighters you are likely to face in your weight division. This is an excellent way to develop a prefight strategy by observing weaknesses a fighter may have.

18. In training, fight an assortment of different fighters: tall, short, slow, fast, aggressive, defensive. Each fighter will offer you a variety of challenges, calling on you to add and subtract tactics from your fight strategy.

19. Always have some idea of what plan to use in the ring, even for a sparring session. These tactics should be discussed thoroughly with your coach prior to any amateur or pro fight.

20. Keep your fight game basic. Do not try any techniques that may look good but cannot get the job done. If a technique can't do damage, don't use it.

A first round 40-second victory over Larry Poore, with a rear leg roundhouse kick to the ribs. Aired on NBC TV, August 11, 1980. Photo by Tom Evans.

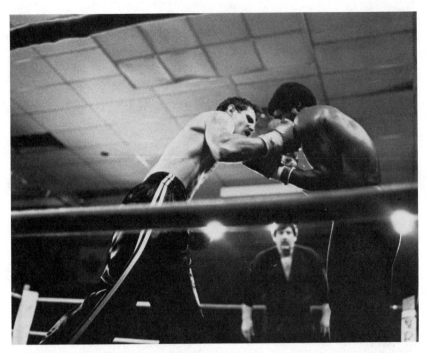

Defeating Glenn McMorris February 1981 in Ottawa, Canada. The win came in the fifth round with a right uppercut to the body. Photo by Tom Evans.

21. Never fear your opponent. If you are in top physical condition and have prepared yourself properly, you will more than hold your own. If your opponent notices that you're afraid, it will make him more aggressive. By carrying yourself into the ring with self-confidence, you will gain respect from your opponent, whether he shows it or not.

22. Strategy and psychology are inseparable. Never let an opponent psych you out, no matter what antics he tries to pull at the weigh-in or in the ring. When you react to his shenanigans, he will know he's getting to you. My psych game is simply to smile prior to the first bell. Smiling and showing no emotion toward my opponent puts him on edge because he's not quite sure what to expect from me.

Your mental attitude as a fighter must be fearless. Photo by Tom Evans.

The stare; playing the psych game. Photo by Myles Burke.

23. To avoid injury, cease all hard sparring one week before a fight and always lay off, except for some light calisthenics, two days before a match.

24. During a match, occasionally execute powerful rear leg roundhouse kicks to your opponent's guard to numb his arms and weaken his defense.

25. Learn from your mistakes. Three losses during the early part of my career did more to build my determination to succeed and will to improve than if they had been victories. When you lose in full-contact karate you really have no one to blame but yourself. Go back to the drawing board with your coach and never make the same mistake twice.

When two fighters of equal ability face each other in the arena, the one with the stronger mental determination to succeed is sure to win. Photo by Tom Evans.

IN CLOSING

In my opinion, the way you carry yourself as a person outside the ring is as important as your strategy in the ring. No matter what position you hold in full-contact karate, whether it be amateur or world title holder, your actions reflect on the sport and everyone involved in it. Although some boasting and chest beating are all part of the fight game, it should not be taken to an extreme that would discredit the sport. When a fighter begins making a spectacle of himself he makes everyone look bad. A disrespectful attitude will make your position, no matter how high, a sour one in the eyes of fellow fighters, promoters, and fans.

Be proud of and confident in your abilities, but at all times try to understand the position you hold and its influence on young fighters who are coming up. The example of sportsmanship you set should be a healthy one that others will be proud to follow. Good ring conduct is often rewarded with victory.

Full-contact karate training not only builds a strong body, but strong character in individuals as well.

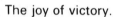

The joy of victory.

JEAN YVES THERIAULT
Fight Record as of May 5, 1982

Opponent	Location	Date	Theriault
1. Serge Simard (Montreal)	Ottawa	June 1976	Won/TKO
2. Murray Sutherland* (Hamilton)	Ottawa	April 1977	Lost/TKO
3. James Louth (Rochester)	Rochester	August 1977	Won/TKO
4. Roger Hurd* (Detroit)	Toronto	September 1977	Won/TKO
5. Mark Kosycki (Detroit)	Ottawa	October 1977	Won/KO
6. Carl Bemon (Philadelphia)	Buffalo	October 1977	Won/Decision
7. Victor Hale (Detroit)	Rochester	November 1977	Won/TKO
8. Mike Chapman (Washington, D.C.)	Ottawa	March 1978	Won/KO
9. Fritz Matthews (Pittsburgh)	Kitchener	March 1978	Won/TKO
10. Robby Warcloud (Moncton)	Sorel	May 1978	Won/TKO
11. Kerry Roop* (Detroit)	Windsor	October 1978	Won/Decision
12. Ralph Hollett* (Halifax)	Ottawa	November 1978	Won/KO
13. Kerry Roop* (Detroit)	Ottawa	April 1979	Won/KO
14. Blinky Rodriguez* (Los Angeles)	Lake Tahoe	May 1979	Lost/KO
15. Emilio Narvaez* (Philadelphia)	Kitchener	June 1979	Won/KO
16. Ace Lewis (Boston)	Boston	July 1979	Won/KO
17. Doug Wear (Boston)	Ottawa	October 1979	Won/KO
18. Doug Wear (Boston)	Boston	November 1979	Won/KO

*Ranked fighters at time of bout.

(continued)

JEAN YVES THERIAULT

Fight Record as of May 5, 1982 (continued)

Opponent	Location	Date	Theriault
19. Ralph Hollett* (Halifax)	Halifax	November 1979	Lost Split Dec.
20. Jeff White (Boston)	Detroit	March 1980	Won KO
21. Ron Thivierge (Rhode Island)	Ottawa	April 1980	Won KO
22. Emilio Narvaez* (Philadelphia)	Boston	July 1980	Won KO
23. Larry Poore* (Sacramento)	Ottawa	August 1980	Won/KO
24. Robert Biggs* (St. Louis)	Ottawa	November 1980	Won TKO
25. Glen McMorris* (Texas)	Ottawa	February 1981	Won KO
26. Rodney Batiste* (Washington, D.C.)	Ottawa	April 1981	Won Decision
27. Eddy Durant (North Carolina)	Ottawa	November 1981	Won TKO
28. Jarvis Gardner* (North Carolina)	Montreal	January 1982	Won TKO
29. Mark Zacharatos* (Los Angeles)	Windsor	February 1982	Won KO
30. Ron Scott (New York)	Ottawa	March 1982	Won TKO
31. Andy Brewer (Milwaukee)	Montreal	April 1982	Won KO
32. Maurice Moore (North Carolina)	Montreal	June 1982	Won KO
33. Tom Richardson (Florida)	Ottawa	September 1982	Won TKO
34. Bernard Clark (Chicago)	London, Ontario	October 1982	Won KO
35. Kerry Roop (Detroit)	Montreal	November 1982	Won TKO

*Ranked fighters at time of bout.

(*Note:* Jean Yves Theriault is still fighting as of this book's publication, and those who wish to see an update of his fight record should write the Professional Karate Association.)

index